D1490636

WELCOME TO KELBURN

This book is an attempt to tell you something about Kelburn and give a brief account of our family history.   Kelburn Castle, unlike most grand houses in Scotland was not planned by an eminent architect like Adams or Lorrimer.   It simply evolved over a period of some 700 years.   As the family became richer or more important, it grew organically.   Over the years, various Earls of Glasgow, or more probably their wives, changed sitting rooms into bedrooms, partitioned rooms to make extra corridors, altered staircases, raised the level of floors and ceilings, moved kitchens from one end of the house to the other and changed the front door from the north to the south side of the house and then back to the north again.   The result is that Kelburn is an eccentric half castle, half-house, always in use and still very much lived-in.

The gardens too have evolved over time and show the horticultural tastes of generations of Earls and Countesses of Glasgow. The Kelburn Glen which starts 800 feet on the hills above and passes just beside the castle has long been admired and during the middle of the 18th century, was often quoted as the most romantic glen in Scotland.

I was not brought up at Kelburn.   In my youth, it was the idyllic place I used to go to stay with my grandparents for part of my holidays. Then it was always a paradise for children, and now that it is my home, I have discovered it is also an inspiration for adults.

I hope some of its magic will rub off on you.

Patrick Boyle, 10th Earl Glasgow

KELBURN CASTLE AND COUNTRY PARK

CONTENTS

KELBURN CASTLE &
A BRIEF HISTORY OF THE BOYLES 4

KELBURN'S GARDENS AND TREES 28

SEASONS IN THE GARDEN 35

THE ICE HOUSE 35

KELBURN GLEN WALKS 44

WILDLIFE IN THE GLEN 52

KELBURN ESTATE 54

THE CENTRE BUILDINGS 58

RIDING AT KELBURN 61

FALCONRY 63

PETS CORNER 63

PLAY AT KELBURN 64

THE SECRET FOREST 66

EVENTS 70

KELBURN CASTLE & A BRIEF HISTORY OF THE BOYLES

Kelburn is thought to be the oldest castle in Scotland to have been continuously inhabited by the same family.   Originally the family name was de Boyville but this changed over the years to Boyle.   The de Boyvilles from Caen in Normandy came over to Britain with William the Conqueror in 1066 and the present branch of the family settled at Kelburn in 1140.

THE DE BOYVILLES SETTLED AT KELBURN IN 1140

THE DE BOYVILLES ARRIVED WITH WILLIAM THE CONQUEROR

BATTLE OF HASTINGS 1066

CAEN, NORMANDY

Sunset over the Islands of Arran, Greater and Little Cumbrae.

The site for the castle would have been chosen for its commanding position overlooking the Firth of Clyde and its close proximity to an ample water supply.

The Kel burn, the mountain stream that passes beside the castle and accounts for its name, rises on the moors 800 feet above and descends to the sea, via a series of waterfalls and deep gorges.

The Kel Burn running below the 1581 castle.

The History of the Boyles at Kelburn is told in a series of idiosyncratic cartoons by Don Aldridge and his exhibition is located within the Centre Buildings.

Nobody knows for certain when a stone building was first constructed on the site, but the original Norman Keep, designed for defence rather than comfort, was probably built by 1200. It was certainly there in 1263 when the Battle of Largs was fought between the Scots and Norwegians on the seashore below Kelburn.

The lower fields of Kelburn estate. This seashore was probably the site of the Battle of Largs.

The original Norman Keep is now enclosed within a grander castle, built in 1581 by the then Laird, John Boyle, at a time when the family was emerging from relative obscurity and beginning to wield some influence within the local community. The 1581 castle can be clearly distinguished from the more recent parts of the building by its two impressive round towers on opposite corners. The 1581 front door, facing south across the burn, is now partly walled up and has become a window. However, it can still be easily identified by the initials carved in stone above the entrance, J.B. and M.C., standing for John Boyle and Marion Crawford, his wife.

SMUGGLING

James I of England (James VI of Scotland) and his successors were constantly in need of money and in 1643 when the English Civil War was underway, the Scots Parliament passed the first ever Scottish Excise Act, which, among other things, imposed a duty of 2s 8d (13p) per Scots pint of whiskey. From then on, smuggling became widespread along the coast of the Firth of Clyde and John Boyle of Kelburn was empowered "to search for, seize and apprehend all Irish victual and cattle, and salt beef made thereof as shall be imported from Ireland, burn any boats or vessels.....and in carrying out these instructions he will not sell any of the victual for his own advantage".

Quoted from 'Clyde Coast Smuggling' by JR.D. Campbell

During the troubled 16th and 17th centuries, the Boyles of Kelburn became wealthy through shipping and shipbuilding. In the later part of the 17th century, the heads of the family involved themselves in Scottish politics and soon became committed to public service.

John Boyle (1636 – 1685), Father of the first Earl of Glasgow, was appointed Commissioner for Supply for Ayrshire and had the unenviable task of trying to stamp out smuggling on the Ayrshire and Renfrewshire coasts. He subsequently became a Crown Commissioner and was given the job of administering, first, all the Bute estates and later all the Argyll estates, when the heads of these families fell foul of the State and their lands were forfeited to the Crown. In the case of the Argyll estates, he found himself in charge of a large part of the Western Highlands and accompanied by troops, rode hundreds of miles over this vast domain collecting money due to the Crown from the tenants of the Earl of Argyll and attempting to sort out the many problems of the inhabitants. He also found time to be a member of the Scottish Parliament representing Ayrshire and Bute.

He was highly respected on both sides of the religious divide in Scotland and destined for greater things, but due maybe to overwork and an over passionate dedication to duty, he died at the relatively young age of 49. However, his distinguished career prepared the way for the ennoblement of his son.

John's son, **David Boyle (1666-1733)** was an influential Scottish statesman, a privy councillor and Lord of the Treasury, and it was he who was created Earl of Glasgow in 1703, one of the last of the Scottish peerages.   He believed it was in Scotland's best interest to join with England and become one United Kingdom under the Stuart Monarch's and he was one of the leading architects of the Act of Union in 1707 which united the English and Scottish parliaments.   He is sometimes charged with being responsible for bribing impoverished Jacobites within the Scottish Parliament to vote for the Union against their natural instincts.   The first Earl was also High Commissioner to the General Assembly of the Church of Scotland and Rector of Glasgow University.   Besides his close association with the University, he was very fond of the city of Glasgow, generally regarded in 1700 (by Daniel Dafoe among others), as a much cleaner and more attractive town than Edinburgh.

II

The 1st Earl of Glasgow's Mansion House, completed in 1700, with the new front door facing north.

This, and the support he received from the city's merchants for championing the Union cause, are the most likely reasons for his choosing the name of Glasgow for his title. It was the First Earl who made the most interesting addition to Kelburn Castle. He planned and ordered a new mansion house to be built and joined to the existing castle, with a new and grander front door facing north (photograph above). It was completed in 1700, and this larger home was now called Kelburn House. (Castles had become unfashionable at the time, regarded as primitive and uncomfortable in comparison with English Stately Homes).

The present large drawing room (opposite above), a double cube, with its high cornice and large sash windows, was originally the grand dining room, and is rated today by many architectural historians as one of the most beautiful rooms in Scotland.

Top: The 1700 drawing room on the first floor with its original large sash windows and (above), a fanciful painting of Kelburn and the immediate estate, at about the same time.

Kelburn Castle c.1730

During the 18th and 19th centuries, the Earls of Glasgow become very considerable landowners. They acquired their land either through legacies from other branches of the Boyle family or through judicious marriages to noble ladies with inheritances of their own. By the time **George Boyle (1775-1843)**, became the **fourth Earl of Glasgow**, they had acquired considerably more land in Ayrshire, the estate of Halkhead outside Paisley, estates in Dunbartonshire, Fife, Northumberland and the greater part of Cumbrae, the island lying directly across the water from Kelburn. All in all, they owned over 120,000 acres in Scotland and, with mineral rights, the fourth Earl collected a yearly rent of £60,000, which was a considerable fortune in those days.

The family's financial troubles began with the **fifth Earl, James Carr Boyle (1792-1869)**, an eccentric and notorious gambler, renowned for his short temper, who established himself as one of the leading figures of the English Turf.   He owned several race horses but refused to give any of them

a name until they had won a race and consistently fired his jockeys when they lost, only to reinstate them the next day.   He was a member of the Jockey Club for 30 years and, although he won the 2000 Guineas shortly before his death, the Derby and St Leger always eluded him; He died without children and was succeeded by his half brother.

When **George Frederick Boyle (1825-1890)**, as sixth Earl of Glasgow, inherited the title in 1869, he also inherited all the Boyle Estates. He ran six large fully staffed residences, Hawkhead at Paisley, Crawford Priory in Fife, the Garrison on the Isle of Cumbrae (which he greatly enlarged), a town house in Perth and Edinburgh and Kelburn itself.

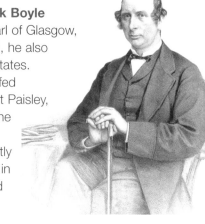

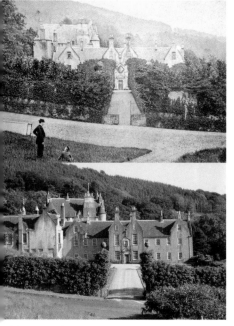

In practice he spent little time at Kelburn, which he regarded as cold and drafty and in the 1870's let it out on a long lease to a prosperous Glasgow merchant, who was responsible for building the Victorian Wing (see left), onto the east side of the castle. The Victorian wing has turned out to be a very useful addition, housing as it still does, the original large kitchen, the billiard room, four extra bedrooms and an impressive dining room overlooking the islands of the Firth of Clyde and retaining by its original Morris wallpaper.

Kelburn Castle (c.1870) before the Victorian wing was added, with a forecourt of laurel bushes and, below, the castle now with its Victorian wing and a lawned forecourt.

The Victorian dining room with its original Morris wallpaper, completed *c*.1885,

and the view from the dining room window.

17

Unfortunately for the Boyle family, the sixth Earl, from early university days, was caught up in the religious controversies of the day, particularly the Oxford movement, and he ran into debt building and endowing Episcopal churches all over Scotland, including a cathedral in Perth and his own particular project, the collegiate church in Millport on the Island of Cumbrae, which later became the Cathedral of the Isles.

Renowned today as the smallest cathedral in Europe, it was designed by Butterfield and cherished as one of Scotland's most important historical buildings. In the view of Scotland's Episcopal Church, the sixth Earl was a great benefactor, something close to a saint, and often referred to as 'the good Earl'.

As far as the Boyles are concerned though, he is the one whose profligacy impoverished and very nearly ruined the family. In 1888, he was in debt to the tune of nearly one million pounds and all his 120,000 acres were put up for auction. He had no male heir and his cousin, David Boyle of Stewarton, later seventh Earl of Glasgow, sold his own estate, Shewalton near Irvine, to raise the money to buy the estates at Kelburn. All the rest was lost to the family.

Contemporary Victorian watercolour of Cumbrae's Cathedral of the Isles, conceived and financed by the 6th Earl and the same Cathedral as it looks today.

THE 7TH
EARL OF
GLASGOW

The **seventh Earl (1833-1915)** who succeeded to
the title in 1890, was made Governor of New
Zealand from 1892 to 1898 and acquired the title of
Baron Fairlie in his own right. He and the eighth
and ninth Earls were all distinguished navel officers.
When not at sea, they spent most of their lives at
Kelburn, ever struggling to find sufficient resources
to keep the castle and the estate maintained.

7th Earl

I've brought you all here to tell you that we are in some financial difficulty but as none of you cost much I shall look after you all and my 14 foresters can make paths in the woods for the Countess. We are going to govern New Zealand for 5 years and let the castle..

WHILE THE EARL GOVERNED NEW ZEALAND...

1893 - All women were given the right to vote, a liquor licensing poll was introduced and banknotes became legal tender.

1894 - Clark, Fyfe and Graham became the first people to climb Mt. Cook, the highest peak on the islands.

1896 - The population grew to 743,214.

1898 - The first cars were imported.

THE GOVERNOR'S HOUSE

The eighth Earl (1874-1963) a Captain in the Royal Navy, inherited in 1915. Due largely to Bolshevik atrocities he witnessed when stationed in Vladivostock after World War One, he grew fanatically fearful of the Communist threat and, for a time led a semi-fascist organisation called the Scottish Loyalists, who, among other acts, felt themselves justified in carrying out raids on the Communist headquarters in Glasgow and stealing all their files. However, in later life, he mellowed and became a respectable and much loved convenor of Ayrshire County Council and a loyal supporter of the war effort in World War Two. In 1941, Kelburn played host to a group of commandos who were billeted here for a few months training. In an exercise, the commandos inadvertently blew out all the windows in the front of the house through a misjudged quantity of explosives. The novelist, Evelyn Waugh, describes this unfortunate incident in one of the most famous letters to his niece.

'So No.3 Cmdo were very anxious to be chums with Lord Glasgow so they offered to blow up an old tree stump for him and he was very grateful and he said don't spoil the plantation of young trees near it because that is the apple of my eye and they said no of course not we can blow a tree down so that it falls on a sixpence and Lord Glasgow said goodness you are clever and he asked them all to luncheon for the great explosion. So Col. Drummond-Slater D.S.O. said to his subaltern, have you put enough explosive in the tree. Yes, sir, 75lbs. Is that enough? Yes sir I worked it out by mathematics it is exactly right. Well better put a bit more. Very good sir.

And when Col. D. Slater D.S.O. had had his port he sent for the subaltern and said subaltern better put a bit more explosive in that tree. I don't want to disappoint Lord Glasgow. Very good sir.

Then they all went out to see the explosion and Col. D.S. D.S.O. said you will hurt no young trees and Lord Glasgow said goodness you are clever.'

So soon they lit the fuse and waited for the explosion and presently the tree, instead of falling quietly sideways, rose 50 feet into the air, taking with it 1/2 acre of soil and the whole of the young plantation.

And the subaltern said Sir I made a mistake, it should have been $7\frac{1}{2}$ lbs not 75.

Lord Glasgow was so upset he walked in dead silence back to his castle and when they came to turn the drive in sight of his castle what should they find but that every pane of glass in the building was broken.

So Lord Glasgow gave a little cry & ran to hide his emotion in the lavatory and there when he pulled the plug the entire ceiling, loosened by the explosion, fell on his head.

This is quite true.   E'

EVELYN WAUGH (1903-1966), WROTE 'DECLINE AND FALL', 'SCOOP' AND 'BRIDESHEAD REVISITED' AMONG MANY OTHER NOVELS.

The **ninth Earl (1910-1984)**, who died at Kelburn, retired as a Rear Admiral, his last post being Flag Officer Malta. He had a distinguished naval and war time career, winning the DSC for his part in the pursuit and sinking of the Bismarck in 1942, when he was Signal Officer on the destroyer, HMS Norfolk.

HMS Norfolk

Imperial War Museum FL 1864

SINKING THE BISMARCK

In May 1941, the German Battleship Bismark, at that time the most formidable fighting ship afloat, escaped into the Atlantic. Her presence posed a fearful threat to the convoys that kept Britain alive. Engaged by two of Britain's battleships, she gravely damaged the Prince of Wales and sunk the Hood, which blew up spectacularly when a shell from the Bismark struck the ship's magazine.

The continuing pursuit of the Bismark by over a dozen British warships covered over two million square miles, ranging from the Baltic to the Atlantic Ocean, and nearly 4000 British and German sailors died. It was one of the great naval battles of the 2nd World War.

The present Earl and his wife Isabel, have two children, David and Alice. Patrick Boyle, 10th Earl of Glasgow worked in the British film industry and later made his name producing television documentaries. While working for Yorkshire Television, he and Isabel

met. They established Kelburn Country Centre in 1977, opening the grounds and gardens to the public on a commercial basis for the first time. The castle is open for guided tours for two months of every year and available for functions and private parties at all times.

The four poster bed in the South Room

KELBURN'S GARDENS AND TREES

Little is known about Kelburn's park or garden before the time of the first Earl, and nearly all the existing trees and features date from after 1700. The great exceptions are the two magnificent yew trees in the walled garden, a male and a female standing side by side, which are certified as over 1,000 years old.

The trunk of one of the two 1,000 year old yew trees

It is humbling to consider that these two stood there before the de Boyvilles ever arrived at Kelburn and one can only wonder who might have planted them.

Karl Brownlee, Kelburn's Head Gardener & Lord Glasgow, under the weeping larch with their awards for Kelburn's Heritage Trees

The pair of Yew trees have been recognised by the Forestry Commission as two of Scotland's 100 most important heritage trees. (Another of Kelburn's Heritage Trees is the Weeping Larch, described on page 40). Some of the Oaks in the Oak wood above the castle and in the lower part of the glen are likely to be four or five hundred years old.

The 1st Earl of Glasgow built the walled forecourt in front of the castle, and this may have been the extent of the formal gardens at Kelburn at the time, although he would certainly have started some tree planting and landscaping on the other sides of his new house. He was also responsible for commissioning two obelisk-shaped sundials, the one below the west side of the castle is a particularly fine specimen, important enough to feature in a Japanese book on 'Sundials of the World'.

LORD GLASGOW STANDING BY
THE FAMOUS SUNDIAL ON THE
WEST ON THE CASTLE.
OBELISK-SHAPED SUNDIALS
ARE RARE AND PECULIAR TO
SCOTLAND. THIS ONE IS
PRIMARILY DECORATIVE AND
MARKS A PERIOD IN EUROPEAN
HISTORY WHEN THE ARTS AND
SCIENCES WERE NOT
REGARDED AS SEPARATE FIELDS
OF STUDY. IT IS OVER 9 FOOT
HIGH AND HAS THE INITIALS
OF THE 1ST EARL AND HIS
FIRST WIFE, LINDSAY
CRAWFORD, WITH THE DATE
1707, ENGRAVED ON IT.

The 'Plaisance'

John, 3rd Earl of Glasgow, (1740-1775) and his wife Elizabeth Ross, a considerable heiress in her own right, clearly loved Kelburn and spent most of their lives here. It was during their time that much planting and landscaping was carried out. The walled garden, known as 'the Plaisance' (French for 'a pleasant place'), was created below the forecourt, with ten-foot walls on three sides, built as a windbreak against the severe westerly gales. The west coast climate however, also brings the rain and relative warmth of the Gulf Stream, making it possible to grow many sub-tropical plants and shrubs.

The upper part of the 'Plaisance'

The 3rd Earl and Countess also set out the Children's Garden, a small formal garden in the shape of the Scottish flag, created for their four children (right), split into four segments with the initials of each child planted in miniature box hedges in the middle corners. These box hedges and initials have been preserved to this day.

The painting by David Martin (c.1770) is of the 3rd Earl's four children, whose initials can still be clearly seen, hedged into the four centre corners of the Children's Garden.

SEASONS IN THE GARDEN

Some Rhododendrons flower in winter. The earliest, Nobeanum, *begins in November and continues into the New Year, when* Christmas Cheer *with its pink flowers takes over. Then in February and March,* Moupinense, Cipinense *and* Thomsonii *with sea green leaves and blood red flowers continue to brighten the winter months. By late January, the banks of the burn by Sanhams Bridge are a sea of* Snowdrops. *By March, the early wild* Daffodils *begin to dominate the landscape and they are followed or joined by the aromatic leaves of* Wild Garlic *with its unmistakable scent which shortly produces a mass of strong white flowers spreading all over the garden. Especially attractive are* Rhododendron Loderi, Fragrantissimum, *with strongly perfumed white flowers, a wonderful 12 foot high* Pieris *with scarlet bracts, and white wax-like* Lily of the Valley *flowers. Particularly striking too are the* Embothrium (Chilean Fire Bush) *with its brilliant scarlet flowers and* Crinodendron Hookerianum *with glowing crimson lanterns, hanging thickly along its branches. July, August and September bring the herbaceous borders in the Plaisance into full flower. Many fascinating plants bloom throughout this period, like the wonderful* Eucryphia Glutinosa, *white flowers with conspicuous stamens, and* Hoheria Glabrata *with masses of fragrant, almost translucent white flowers.* Weinmannia Trichosperma *is a very attractive South American shrub with pinnate, fern-like leaves. The white flowers are produced in the dense racemes, but the real delight are the small, copper-red seed vessels that follow the flowering.*

THE ICE HOUSE

The Ice House at Kelburn, which lies fifty yards below the castle and overlooks the burn, was only re-discovered in 1985, when excavations started on what was thought to be an old parapet. This Ice House must have been in use in Victorian times but no-one knows when it was first built. The earliest recorded ice house in Britain is at Green Park, London, and dated 1660. They were carefully constructed chambers under the ground where large blocks of ice could be stored for use in the big house, presumably for keeping meat fresh and cold drinks cold.

As at Kelburn, ice houses were often oval shaped, fifteen or so feet deep, covered over at the top and entered by steps leading down from the side. The blocks of ice were brought in the winter and stored in the ice house with straw separating one layer of blocks from the one below. At the bottom is a drain to allow the melted ice to run away.

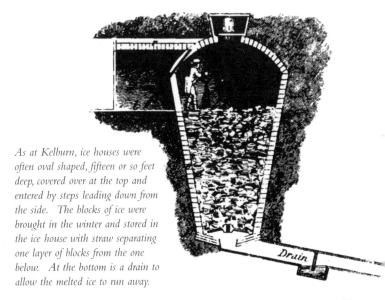

By the middle of the 18th century, the Kelburn Glen already had a reputation as a place of romance and beauty, and on the 3rd Earl's death, his wife, the Countess, commissioned Robert Adam to design a monument to his memory in one of the glen's beauty spots. The monument (which cost her £300 in 1776) has a poetic inscription, that is a touching tribute to a man she so clearly loved and admired:

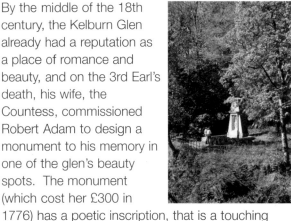

Sacred to the Memory of JOHN Earl of GLASGOW, whose exalted Piety and liberal sentiments of Religion, Unfettered by systems, and Joined with universal Benevolence, were as singular as that Candour and Modesty which cast a pleasing veil over his Distinguished Abilities. His Loyalty and Courage he Exerted in the Service of his Country in whose cause he Repeatedly Suffered with Fortitude and Magnanimity. At the Battle of Fontenoy Early in Life he lost his Hand, and his Health, His Manly Spirit, not to be subdued, at Lafeld he received Two Wounds in one attack. To Perpetuate the Remembrance of a Character so Universally Beloved and admired, and to animate his Children to the Imitation of his Estimable Qualities This Humble Monument is Erected by his Disconsolate Widow. Ob. 7 May 1775.

Their son, George Boyle, fourth Earl of Glasgow (1865-1843), whose initials LGB are clearly hedged in the Children's Garden, must have introduced many new trees to Kelburn because so many of the woods, copses and individual trees were planted between 1780 and 1843.   Avenues and copses of 200 year old beech trees abound all over the park and several impressive silver firs of that age are still standing firm in the glen.

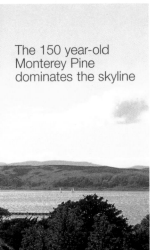

The 150 year-old
Monterey Pine
dominates the skyline

One of Kelburn's most impressive trees is the Monterey Pine,
about 150 years old, beside the tennis court, which towers
above all others in the garden area. It is reckoned to be the
tallest and oldest Monterey Pine in Scotland and, in spite of
considerable storm damage to the branches over the years,
it has proved able to withstand wind speeds too strong
for neighbouring trees.

The unique Weeping Larch

Larch and Sycamore were introduced to Scotland in the eighteenth century and there is a unique specimen of each in the garden.

The most remarkable of all the trees at Kelburn is the Weeping Larch, which spreads over about a quarter of an acre between the tennis court and the Plaisance. It is thought to be about 180 years old and is like no other. Its branches grow out in all directions, travelling sometimes upwards again and sometimes along the ground like a snake. Some of the branches have fused into other branches and, unless closely inspected, it is difficult to believe that this great monster is in fact all one tree.

Although many Sycamores turn into scrubby or twisted trees and are particularly unfashionable nowadays, the one at the top of the bank above Sanham's Bridge is one of the most aesthetically pleasing trees at Kelburn, with its beautifully wide and rounded canopy and the abundance of moss and ferns that live within it.

Other interesting trees have been planted more recently. The clump of Wellingtonias with their great height and soft red bark, fashionable in the middle of the last century, date from about 1850 and are near the Stockade close to the Centre buildings. Two Cedars of Lebanon stand by the side of the road at the bottom of the garden and there is a Japanese Cedar in the middle of the lower part of the Plaisance, weather-damaged and looking like a giant Bonsai tree.

The Sycamore, with the castle in the background

Cordyline Australis

When the 7th Earl of Glasgow returned from New Zealand in 1897, he and the Countess brought back a number of trees and shrubs from the South Pacific, many of which seem to thrive in this climate.

Unusual trees or shrubs were often planted to commemorate an event. A fine Turkey Oak below the New Zealand Garden was planted by the late ninth Earl of Glasgow (aged one!) to celebrate the Coronation of George V and Queen Mary, who was his Godmother. The gate in the north wall of the Plaisance has a large 'G' set in it and is known as the Golden Gate because it was given by the staff to the eighth Earl and Countess of Glasgow in 1956 to commemorate their Golden Wedding Anniversary. In 1984, Karl Brownlee, Kelburn's Head Gardener planted a Pocket Handkerchief (Davida Involucrata) Tree in memory of the ninth Earl and Countess of Glasgow who both died in the same year. Most recently, in 1991, Dame Te Ata-i-Rangikaahi, the Maori Queen, planted and blessed a Lancewood Tree in the New Zealand Garden to mark her visit to Kelburn.

Yucca Filamentosa Variegata
with the Japanese Cedar in
the background

43

KELBURN GLEN WALKS

One of Kelburn's most outstanding features is its glen. In the space of just over half a mile, the Kel burn, which has helped to form the glen over thousands of years, rises on the moors 800 feet above the castle and drops dramatically, by way of many waterfalls and deep gorges, to the sea. The glen is a wealth of wild flowers and ferns, shrubs and trees, partly cultivated but predominantly wild.

Near the bottom, 300 yards from the centre buildings, is the Waterfall Pool. At this point, the burn drops a sheer 20 feet into a spectacular grotto surrounded on three sides by overhanging cliffs of red and yellow sandstone. The pool below is small but deep and traps many sea trout that are unable to make further progress up the burn.

The 18th century stone bridge at the top of the glen is the Bow Brig and the footbridge at the bottom is Sanham's Bridge. The bridge over the waterfall pool is called the Kelburn Bridge, with the three most recent bridges being the New, the Three Falls and the Martindale Bridge (see page over).

Opposite: The Waterfall Pool

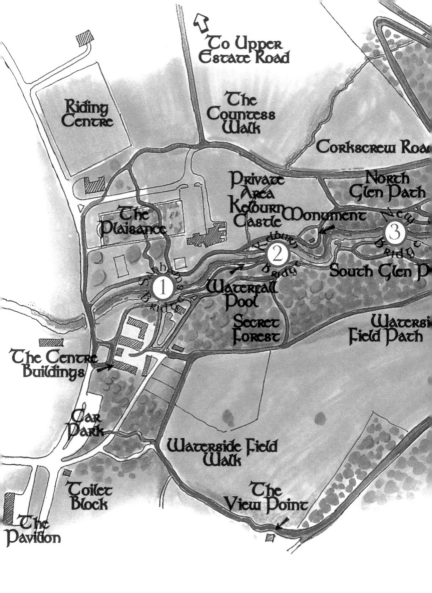

To Upper Estate Road

Riding Centre

The Countess Walk

Corkscrew Road

Private Area
Kelburn Castle

Monument

North Glen Path

The Plaisance

② ③

South Glen Path

Waterfall Pool

Secret Forest

Waterside Field Path

The Centre Buildings

① Stables Bridge

Car Park

Waterside Field Walk

Toilet Block

The View Point

The Pavilion

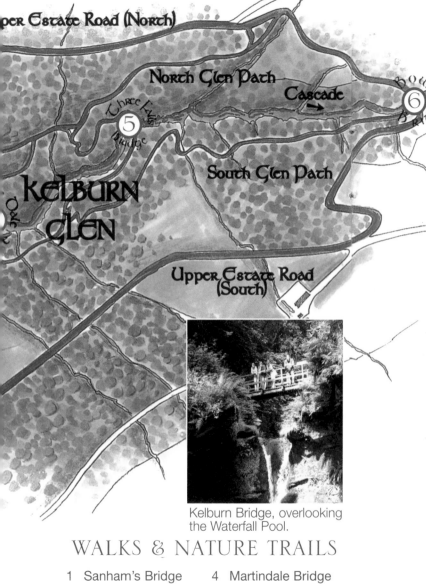

Upper Estate Road (North)

North Glen Path

Cascade

Three Falls Bridge

⑤

Bow Brig

⑥

KELBURN GLEN

South Glen Path

Oak ?

Upper Estate Road (South)

Kelburn Bridge, overlooking
the Waterfall Pool.

WALKS & NATURE TRAILS

1 Sanham's Bridge
2 Kelburn Bridge
3 New Bridge
4 Martindale Bridge
5 Three Falls Bridge
6 Bow Brig

47

1. The Garden and Historical Walk

For those who like historic gardens and are interested in trees and Kelburn's features of special interest, a short circular walk has been marked out with explanatory signboards placed at appropriate points along the route (see map in back pocket). Starting from the signboard above the Centre Buildings, it takes you by the Museum, over Sanham's Bridge, past the Children's Garden, the Ice House and on to the Monument. It then leads down the Corkscrew Road, beside the Oak Wood, round to the front of Kelburn Castle and into the Plaisance and other parts of the garden, where many of Kelburn's most interesting trees and shrubs can be found, before returning back over Sanham's Bridge. The whole trip is about a quarter of a mile long. A leaflet to accompany the History Trail, giving more detail on Kelburns' history and features of interest can be obtained from the Information Office.

2. THE SHORT GLEN WALK (OR SCULPTURE TRAIL)

Although all the glen walks involve a certain amount of uphill walking and climbing steps, the short glen walk is the more gentle and least precipitous and follows a route up the South Glen path from the Centre, over the New Bridge and down by the North Glen path past the Monument. The walk is about half a mile long, takes a leisurely forty minutes and is recommended for older visitors and families. Regrettably, however, it is not suitable for wheelchairs, and parents pushing child buggies may find some of it hard going.

Along the route of the short glen walk is a succession of wooden sculptures in the shape of animals, birds and fish that can be found on Kelburn Estate. The trail starts with a fox at the viewpoint above the pond overlooking the Castle and ends with a hare on the corner above Sanham's Bridge. There are ten other wooden creatures to discover and a children's quiz sheet relating to the sculptures can be obtained at the Information Office to make the trail more stimulating for those children who usually resist going for walks.

Animal sculptures on the Sculpture Trail, carved by Alan Lees

3. The Middle Glen Walk (via Three Falls Bridge)

For the Middle Glen Walk, carry on up the South Glen Path (passing the turning to the New Bridge) and cross the burn by the Three Falls Bridge. The path joins the North Glen Path by a grassy plateau of Beech trees where seats have been set. From there you can descend to the Centre by way of the New Bridge or carry on down to the Castle past the Monument or leave the Glen altogether by taking the Corkscrew Road into the Gardens.

4. The Long Glen Walk (via the Bow Brig)

For those with sufficient energy the Long Glen Walk takes you right up to the top of the Glen. One hundred and fifty yards from the top in the South side is a lovely 30 foot waterfall, simply called 'the cascade', and at the point where the path meets the Upper Estate Road, there is the Bow Brig which overlooks a series of rocky pools of running water. Once on the Upper Estate Road there are some magnificent views looking across to the islands in the Firth of Clyde. It is advisable on this walk to ascend by the South Glen Path and come down by the North Glen Path, which is much steeper.

5. THE COUNTESS WALK AND UPPER ESTATE ROAD

Some of the best views at Kelburn can be had from the Countess Walk which leads uphill on a gentle incline from the front of the Castle to the Estate Road. From there, you can walk on level ground round the Upper Estate Road and either return by one of the glen paths or carry on to the viewpoint and back to the Centre by the path through the Waterside Field. This is a picturesque two hour walk, full of variety that gives the visitor a good general impression of Kelburn Estate.

51

Photo: Mark Hamblin

DIPPER

WILDLIFE IN THE GLEN

The Glen is the home for a great variety of wildlife.
Throughout the year you may see Roe Deer, Foxes,

Squirrels and the occasional
Hedgehog darting out of sight.
Grey herons often glide up the
Glen to land beside the burn.
Dippers may be seen perching
on rocks whilst Buzzards circle
overhead.   During the winter, large flocks of small birds
foraging can be seen, such as Long Tail Tits, Siskins and
Goldcrests and Bullfinches are often seen feeding down
by the Waterfall Pool.   By spring, Swallows and
Housemartins are regular visitors to the Glen, and
Woodpeckers may be heard drumming in the woods.
Early summer heralds the migrant visitors including the
Willow Warbler and the distinctive sounding Chiffchaff.

In mid January Snowdrops start to appear and by
spring, Bluebells, Wood Sorrel and Wood Anemone are
all in flower early before the trees grow their leaves.
Throughout the summer there is a succession of
flowering plants to see in the Glen, Wild Strawberry,
Wild Raspberry, Red Campion and Herb Robert are
just a few you might find.   Most notable of the non-
flowering plants are the Ferns of which there are several
varieties including Harts Tongue and Male Fern.

KELBURN ESTATE

Kelburn Estate covers an area of over 3,500 acres, starting at the edge of the sea and rising to a height of 1,300 feet.   Two thousand acres is rough moorland, for grazing sheep and cattle, and 1,500 acres of the better land is contained with a seven foot wall that encircles the heart of the estate. There are two farms, 150 acres of agricultural land on the lower ground, 300 acres of planted woodland, 150 acres of amenity wood (which includes the glen) and 40 acres of park and garden (which includes the area around the centre buildings).

There are two tenant farmers and Kelburn's permanent staff consists of an Estate Manager, a Gardener, a Gamekeeper, a Shop Manager, a Café Manager, a Commercial Manager for the Castle, an Estate Accountant, two full-time Rangers, a Head Groom and her assistants, an Office Manager and two Secretary/Receptionists. During the height of the tourist season though, over three times that number are employed on a seasonal or part-time basis to manage to Country Centre. There are twelve houses or cottages on the estate, several of which are occupied by Kelburn employees.

The Castle, gardens and some of the outbuilding *c*.1950. The kitchen garden in the foreground has now been converted into Kelburn's riding centre.

By contrast, at the turn of the 19th century, Kelburn's outside staff consisted of eight foresters, five gardeners, a joiner, a carter, two dairymaids, three laundrymaids and a shepherd.

All the farms were tenanted at that time too, so the main duty of the shepherd was to ensure that the tenant's sheep did not stray onto the policies. The staff were employed to provide for the castle, keep the estate maintained and make sure the gardens looked good. Any income that could be derived from owning an estate was acquired through rents from tenants.

It was the eighth Earl of Glasgow who started to plant and grow trees commercially at Kelburn, starting in the early 1920's. This policy was continued by the 9th Earl who became passionate and very knowledgeable about trees. In the late '60s, the coverts of Larch and Sitka Spruce, mixed with hardwoods that had been sensitively planted and systematically thinned, were greatly admired by tree lovers and forestry experts all over Scotland. Tragically, in the winter of 1969 'Hurricane Queenie' made its way across the Atlantic and struck the west of Scotland with unparalleled force resulting in over 60 acres of Kelburn's woodlands being flattened and considerable damage being caused elsewhere. Nowadays, sadly, forestry is no longer a profitable industry for estate owners and it is unlikely that the Kelburn woods will ever be so well tended again.

The horses' field in front of the castle

THE CENTRE BUILDINGS

The old Home Farm, now converted into the Centre Buildings, as it is today, and as it was c.1950

The buildings that now form the central square of the Country Centre were built about 1760. They used to form the Home Farm and were fully operational up until the First World War. Besides housing farm animals, they were the living and working place of many estate and domestic workers and their families. The buildings included a stable, a byre, a piggery, a henhouse, a laundry, a wash house, a dairy (providing milk and butter for the Castle), a joiners' shop, a sawmill, four houses for estate workers and rooms on the top floor which were sleeping quarters for the milkmaids and dairymaids.

Before the opening of Kelburn Country Centre, most of the buildings had fallen into disuse. In converting them, every attempt was made to conserve their original character. The old stables, which used to house the carthorses, have been turned into a tearoom with the old stalls and stone floor retained. The old laundry and wash house is now the gift shop and one of the estate cottages is the café and ice cream shop. The joiners' shop and part of an estate cottage has become the reception area, while another estate cottage is again fully lived in. Other cottages have become offices and the room where the milkmaids and dairymaids used to sleep is now a flat.

The old byre is now the home of Don Aldridge's Cartoon Exhibition, the old hen house is now a pottery workshop, and the old midden, in the centre of the square, where farm rubbish used to be collected, has been paved and set out with tables and chairs for visitors to eat and drink.

Above the Centre Buildings is what used to be a curling pond before the First World War and which has been converted into and ornamental duck pond. (It is interesting to note how much colder winters were in those days).   At its far end is the Museum. This was built by the seventh Earl of Glasgow when he returned from New Zealand in 1898 to house all the curios and artefacts he had collected in the South Pacific.   Some still remain and the museum today also contains an interesting exhibition of photographs showing the governor's experiences and activities while he was serving in New Zealand, and a selection of farm and domestic implements dating from the turn of the century that have been collected from all over Kelburn Estate.

The corregated iron Musuem with the pond in the foreground

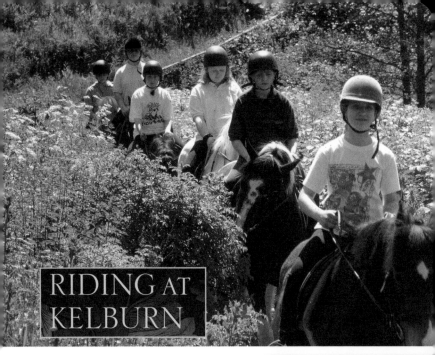

RIDING AT KELBURN

Pony Trekking was introduced the first year Kelburn Country Centre opened, using only ponies hardy enough to spend the whole year out in the fields. But, as stables and other buildings were erected to keep horses, Kelburn has developed into a fully fledged Riding Centre.   The old North Stables, which had been abandoned as a

storeroom for seventy years, gradually came back to life again and beside the North Stables, an arena has been established for jumping and riding lessons.   As Kelburn now also provides livery for client's horses, there could be anything up to fifty horses on Kelburn Estate at any one time.

FALCONRY

Since 1995, several different falconers have made
their home at Kelburn and we presently have a
large falconry centre with over 26 different birds of
prey, including Kestrels, Hawks, Snowy and Eagle
owls, Peregrine Falcons and Steppe Eagle.
Falconry demonstrations take place on most days
during the season.

PETS' CORNER

Because animals of all sorts are indigenous to
farms and woodlands, a Pets Corner seems to
have evolved naturally at Kelburn.   Over the years
there have been goats (large, pigmy and mountain),
chipmonks, sheep (black-faced and Jacob), pigs
(farmyard and Vietnamese pot-bellied), stoats,
weasels, hedgehogs (which could never be
contained), foxes (particularly Sacha, a tame fox
owned by an ex-Head Ranger, Nina Finnegan),
chickens (including some rare Buff Pekins), birds of
all sorts and a never-ending variety of rabbits and
guinea pigs.   Recently we have had to reduce the
number of animals in Pet's corner.   Law relating to
children coming in contact with livestock have
become stricter and the public are now more
sensitive and critical about animals in captivity.
Needless to say, great care is taken over the
welfare of all our pets.

PLAY AT KELBURN

Kelburn's Sawmill provides our own timber so most of Kelburn's play areas are home made.   The Adventure Course above the Ranger Centre was started in 1978 with help from the Royal Marines as a challenge for children.   It has been improved and upgraded every year.   The Stockade, which stands beside the Sawmill, was completed in 1980 with smaller children in mind. It is a cross between a Wild West Fort and a POW camp with a children's playground in the middle.   . Beyond the pavilion car park is a third children's play area, with swings and other challenges, including the ever popular cableway ride.

The Adventure Course

The Stockade

The Indoor Playbarn

Unlike most play areas in visitor attractions which come ready made by the manufacturers, KELBURN'S PLAYBARN is uniquely designed, themed as a country landscape, beautifully painted by local artist, Ann Cromack, with a castle set on top of a cliff and a maze of caves underneath. A decorative bridge takes you over the ball pool into the caves, a climbing wall helps you scale the cliff, unless you prefer to find your way into the castle via the secret stairway hidden

within the caves. A choice of two slides – a vertical drop or a more gentle descent into the balls – send you rapidly down the 'waterfalls' to ground level again. There is also a small soft play area for young children.

THE SECRET FOREST

Conceived by the present Earl in 1993, the Secret Forest is a magical place for adults and children to explore and discover. Every year will see new features and improvements to old ones. Like the natural trees and shrubs already there, the man-made structures too will grow and change and give birth to even more surprises.

Chinese Garden, with summer house decorated with genuine Chinese paintings!

Gingerbread House, guarded by a witch that has Hanzel and Gretal in a cage hanging from the ceiling!

Stone Grotto with water and a swamp full of crocodiles!

Wooden Maze - the lair of the Green Man!

Oak log Woodcutter's House with secret passage to the Dwarf's House!

The Goblin's Castle with no entrance! Or is there?

35 foot Pagoda with views across the whole of the Forest!

The one big feature so far not completed is the Giant's Castle, which, in its half-finished state is the first thing you see when you enter the Forest.

Besides the buildings, the Secret Forest is home to hundreds of smaller features, some within buildings but most set in appropriate spots along the edges of the paths, including the Prisoner in the Cell, the Celtic Totem Poles, the Time Man, the twelve animals of the Chinese calendar, the Cobra, the Fairy Tree House, the animals of the Wild Wood, the Monster in the Grotto and the Giant Bird sitting on its nest twelve foot above the Crocodile Swamp. Many professional and amateur artists and sculptors have contributed to the Secret Forest, but the majority of wooden sculptures are the work of Alan Lees and the majority of paintings by Ann Cromack.

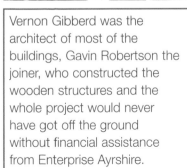

Vernon Gibberd was the architect of most of the buildings, Gavin Robertson the joiner, who constructed the wooden structures and the whole project would never have got off the ground without financial assistance from Enterprise Ayrshire.

KELBURN

CASTLE

AND

COUNTRY

CENTRE

EVENTS AT KELBURN

Every year, Kelburn puts on a number of special events. In the 1990s, large scale events took place such as the Festival of Flight, the Woodcraft and Forestry Fair and the Game Fair with its dog shows, clay pigeon shooting and horse trials. In the summer holidays, there were family events such as Alice in Wonderland and Wizard of Oz weeks and during the Viking Festival in early September, Kelburn presented its own light-hearted theatrical version of the Legend of the Ring, the story immortalised by Wagner's operas. But, because of the high cost of staging these attractions and the dependence on good weather for their success, Kelburn has recently resorted to more modest events managed by the ranger service – Rustic Highland Games, Mini Beast Weekend, Save the Planet Week, etc – which seem just as popular with visitors. However, we still hold a New Zealand Weekend to commemorate the Family's connection with that country and a Viking Day to coincide with the

Largs Viking Festival, and every year in late October, the rangers organise a Halloween Trail in which visitors get to meet ghosts and witches and other legendary monsters.

Also, major companies and Events Organisers continue to use Kelburn as a location for their own events. Scout and Girl Guide Jamborees, Rocket Weekends, 'It's a Knockout' and the Karimoor Mountain Marathon, which attracted nearly 3000 competitors, are a few examples. For the last few years, the Chapterhouse Theatre Company has performed a Shakespeare play in the Castle forecourt on an evening in July.

Kelburn Castle itself is the venue for a number of functions yearly, including dinner parties, weddings and corporate entertaining, often accompanied by pipers and traditional Scottish dancers and musicians.

All Castle enquiries, telephone **01475 568595** or visit **www.kelburncastle.com**

NOTES

Flowers of Kelburn

Rhododendrons:
Nobeanum
Christmas Cheer
Moupinense
Cipinense
Thomsonii
Loderi
Fragrantissimum

Snowdrops
Bluebells
Daffodils
Wild Garlic
Pieris
Lily of the Valley
Embothrium (Chilean Fire Bush)
Crinodendron Hookerianum
Eucryphia Glutinosa
Hoheria Glabrata
Weinmannia Trichosperma

NOTES

TREES OF KELBURN

MONTEREY PINE

LARCH

SYCAMORE

WEEPING LARCH

WELLINGTONIA

CEDAR OF LEBANON

WILDLIFE

JAPANESE CEDAR

TURKEY OAK

ROE DEER

FOXES

POCKET HANDKERCHIEF TREE

SQUIRRELS

LANCEWOOD TREE

HEDGEHOG

GREY HERONS

DIPPERS

BUZZARDS

LONG TAIL TITS

SISKINS

GOLDCRESTS

BULLFINCHES

SWALLOWS

HOUSEMARTINS

WILLOW WARBLER

CHIFFCHAFF

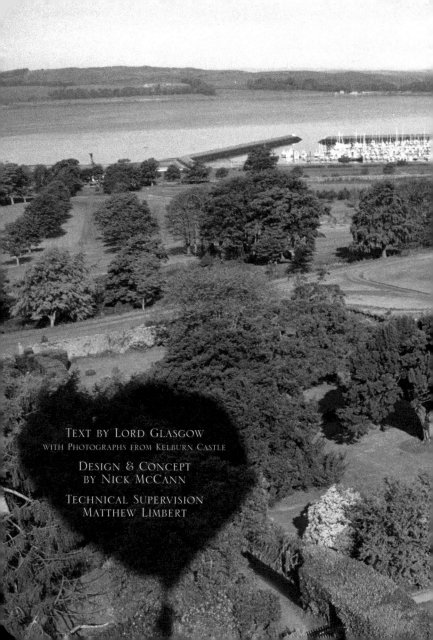

Text by Lord Glasgow
with Photographs from Kelburn Castle

Design & Concept
by Nick McCann

Technical Supervision
Matthew Limbert

Kelburn Castle
and
Country Centre

Wildlife and the Kelburn Glen

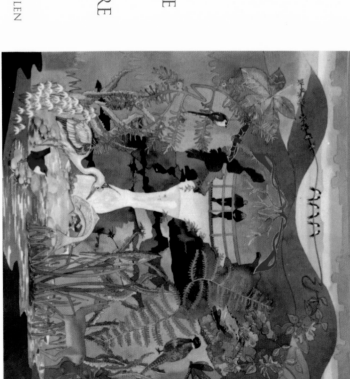

KELBURN CASTLE
AND
COUNTRY CENTRE

The Kelburn Glen by Ann Cromack

Designed and produced by Heritage House Group Ltd. email: publications@hhgroup.co.uk

Published by Heritage House Group Ltd.
Heritage House   Lodge Lane   Derby   DE1 3HE
Tel: 01332 347087   Fax: 01332 290688   email: publications@hhgroup.co.uk
© Heritage House Group Ltd. 2006